LIVING WITH TEENERS

LIVING WITH TEENERS

Grace Sloan Overton

BROADMAN PRESS
Nashville, Tennessee

Broadman Press
Nashville, Tennessee
Twelfth Printing

422-029

Printed in the United States
2-5AL665

To
Richard and Mary
who are living
with their
growing-up children

INTRODUCTION

Here is a book parents have long wanted—something to help them understand their growing-up children. Adolescence introduces diverse crosscurrents which make the rapidly developing child an enigma to himself and an unceasing concern to his parents. The subject of this volume will find an eager response in every father and mother of a teener.

The book pleads for an understanding of these growing-up children. There are factors—physical, emotional, social, spiritual—which the mature parent can understand. For that understanding, parents themselves first of all need to be well-balanced, for, as the author points out, it is too much to ask boys and girls in their developing years to handle their own emotions and those of their parents also. Parents who exercise such discipline of their own emotions and apply themselves in an earnest effort to understand their children will find rich rewards as their children develop through these fleeting years to maturity.

Dr. Overton is eminently qualified for the task in hand. She has given her lifetime to work with young people and their parents. Her work in this field has been through church organizations, on college campuses, on the lecture platform, in private counseling, and through her writings, which have appeared in a number of magazines and in book form.

Dr. Overton devotes approximately half of her time to public engagements which take her to every section of the nation. She is a mother and a grandmother.

This book was first introduced as a series in *Home Life*. The editor is happy that Broadman Press in recognition of the permanent value of Dr. Overton's contribution has enlarged the usefulness of the series through book publication. The challenge of intelligent parenthood will no doubt receive new impetus in the life of every father and mother who read this volume.

JOE W. BURTON
Editor, Home Life

PREFACE

For many years it has been my rare privilege to be associated with teeners. These associations have been varied. We have been together in college classrooms, in summer camps, in youth conferences, in my consulting room in a downtown church, and in the varied activities of church youth programs. Teenagers have listened kindly when I spoke from the platform; they have co-operated fully in discussion groups and forums; they have been forthright as they talked over personal problems with me in confidence.

As the years of this association lengthened, another group of persons played an ever-increasing part in it—*their parents*. More and more parents consulted me on the problems their teeners presented. Teeners themselves, I found, were often unable to understand their parents—their ways of thinking and feeling. Thus there often developed feelings of strain between these growing-up personalities and their already-grown-up adult parents.

It became clear that this sense of tension was a common experience of both parents and their offspring. I felt that the tension was often unnecessary. I saw how often it was permitted to grow rather than being relaxed. I observed how it sometimes put lasting distance between parent and child, even to the point of developing animosities where understanding and mutual regard and affection should have been the ruling feelings between them. And I learned that some of the most regrettable crises in the affairs of families grew out of just such tensions—tensions with simple beginnings, tensions that "sweet reasonableness" and yielding at the right time might have done away with before they had done lasting hurt.

Why do I write these pages? That good parents may the better learn their own skills in living with their teeners, the children God has given them. That they may see their teeners' viewpoint before they speak the possibly too harsh words. That they may learn how their own teeners show those first signs of tension. That they may learn how to avoid all possible strain between themselves and those they love more than their own lives.

Whatever else the teener is, he is a discoverer. He is discovering his own growing personality—his own enlarging world of persons and things. And he profits most from those adults who impress him as meeting him on his own ground. He grows by trying to do the things he finds he can do. He develops skills in getting along with others by making *successful* contacts with others.

But no matter how exciting a teener's life outside his home may be, he always needs to have "back home" mature, levelheaded, sound, settled, helpful, promotive, understanding, sympathetic, and completely adult parents. He needs parents who stay "on an even keel" when his ambitions outrun his capacities; parents to be a "city of refuge" when he has run afoul any safety sign of the adult world—that new, big, wonderful world in which he is for the first time finding his way around!

Thus it comes that teeners *discover the real stuff* of which their parents are made. To them there must come times when we, their parents, seem to stand in the way of their own self-realization. And they may not conceal their discovery from us; for they have not yet learned the gentle art of "making allowance" as have our friends of greater years. It is in such situations—the everyday routine in family living!—that teeners learn the "ins and outs" of their parents' characters. That, too, is discovery.

And of all the discoveries teeners make, none is more important than this: that they shall find in their parents what teeners most need to find there—not wealth alone—or family—standing or profession—or convictions alone. Any or all of these perhaps. But also they must find never-failing love, dependable understanding, overcoming patience. This adds up to *emotional* security—safety at home—in the shelter parents can best supply, and parents alone.

Good parents, these pages are written for you. Should minister or teacher or adviser or leader of youth find any page of help, that will make me glad. But the book is still yours, parents of teeners. It comes into your hands bearing with it a devout prayer. Your sons and daughters will someday look back and count up what they discovered in their teens. In those years potent with promise, bounded around with threatening dangers, may they recall that you were always the strong senior partners in their discoveries! May they declare that you were the sort of parents who mastered the fine art of "living with teeners!"

GRACE SLOAN OVERTON

Adams, New York

CONTENTS

I

OUR EARLY-TEENERS AT HOME

I am sure you have looked at your twelve-year-old daughter while she was "telling you off" (in other words, being saucy) and have thought wistfully, "She's no longer my little girl." Or your husband has said of your twelve- or thirteen-year-old Junior, "What ails him? Is he getting too big for his breeches? *He* needs to be taken down a peg or two!"

You are both aware that something has happened. The scolding, the laying-down-the-law, the coddling—these used to do a little good, but now they no longer work. Your Julia becomes opinionated. Your John gets a bit moody now and then. And you begin to see you are now living with a half-man, half-child person—with a person acting like a young woman who knows more than you. They move about in your house, and you are simply bound to get in the way of each other now and then.

Parents, teachers, and youth leaders are asking many more questions about the adolescent boy and girl. They want to know what are the physical and psychological changes going on and what difference do these changes make? Understanding the adolescent boy and girl is a *must* with parents. I deal with so many boys and girls to whom loving parents have done horrible things just because they didn't understand what was happening physically to their growing-up children.

Said a baffled mother, "Sometimes I think this adolescence is a disease like the mumps, measles, or chickenpox—something our children must go through with and get over!"

But actually adolescence is not a disease—not at all. It is a normal and promising period of growing up. Indeed it is so normal that the child has no sense of "going through with it." It is rather the parents who are baffled and perplexed. As a bright thirteen-year-old girl said, "I think my mother would like me to skip all the fun of being young."

There is nothing strange or weird about adolescence. It begins with a development of the body growing into a body capable of reproducing its kind, of being a parent. This capacity for parenthood is one of the greatest dignities of the body. When one realizes how few adolescents are really taught what this development means to them, one wonders that there is as much virtue and common decency among youth as there is.

It is estimated that less than 25 per cent of adolescents are given any instruction as to the importance of their growing-up bodies. They get lectured and teased but are seldom instructed.

Sometime ago I watched about three hundred junior high school girls react to Walt Disney's film on reproduction and the girl's share in it. It was a clean, healthy reaction. Afterward I asked, "How many of you girls have ever understood what was happening to you as you grew up?" Much less than

25 per cent of them held up their hands. One girl asked, "Why don't our mothers talk to us about a thing as important as this?"

I had about four hundred growing boys together. There was some giggling. So I asked, "Boys, what's so funny?" One boy replied, "Boys and girls." Then I asked, "Boys, did any of you ever hear why and how you were born boys?" There was no more giggling but interest instead. I then told them that when they were conceived their sex was determined; they were to be men. They were born boy-babies with male organs so that they might someday become fathers. That they were now growing up and becoming men. Then I asked, "Boys, what's so funny about that?"

"Nothing," one boy responded, "only I never heard it before."

Another boy said, "All I ever heard was dirt."

And another, "Oh, I've heard a lot of pretty talk about it but never anything that helped much."

And then came once more the question, "Why aren't we told by our parents about this?"

By the age of thirteen boys and girls should accept their sex and what it means to them. Every girl should know that she is a potential mother, what her share in parenthood is, and what she has at stake. Every boy should understand that he is developing the capacity to be a father and what is expected of him as an American boy and man. It is sad beyond expression that our American parents have not been trained to give their children this understanding help.

As I have seen the tragic mistakes of youth just because they were confused and didn't know their own dignity of body and the sacred responsibility to protect this capacity for parenthood, I have been ashamed that we in America have been so very negligent in our responsibility to our children.

Along with this capacity for parenthood, it is only natural that there should come an increased sense of the importance of self. This brings hunger for greater social experience and a demand for recognition. The adolescent's world seems so small, his social opportunities so inadequate, when compared with his hungers and urges to grow up and actually to live.

There are wide individual differences in the age at which adolescence actually begins. Climate, nutrition, type of body and glands—these all play important parts.

Adolescence tends to come to girls earlier than to boys. But somewhere near the age of twelve, the average boy and girl begins to show some evidences of adolescence. The reproductive organs begin to develop. With this there comes an increase of general activity as the secretions of the pituitary, thyroid, and adrenal glands influence growth, digestion, and emotional energy. There comes a spurt of growth, particularly of arms and legs, and enlargement of knees and elbows. With this the veins and arteries do not keep pace for a time; hence, the cold and sweaty hands and feet.

Often the adolescent seems mostly hands and feet.

The gravy ladle spills. The glass of water upsets. The rug gets in the way of shuffling feet. And the resulting embarrassment and self-consciousness only serve to increase the awkwardness. To nag or tease about it does no good. It may build hostility toward the teaser or cause adolescents to withdraw from the social contacts that should normally be theirs.

I suppose there is no hunger for food quite as urgent as that of an adolescent! It sometimes appears the boy doesn't have a stomach to be filled but rather a "regular bureau drawer to keep stuffed." He likes exotic food, dramatic food, and lots of it.

Sometimes girls become very dramatic about their eating or have *notions* about their food. They may mince along with their food at the table, thus dramatizing themselves. One mother told me of her concern about her daughter's apparent slight appetite at the table until one day she came unexpectedly upon her at the open refrigerator door gorging herself ravenously. Then she understood and worried no more.

The physical changes at adolescence sound simple. But they bring a new sense of importance; they result in hunger for new and enlarged social experiences; they produce new demands for recognition of rights. And these often make the period one of conflict between adolescents and their parents. For the new and compulsive sense of self-importance in the adolescent is very hard on the ego of his parents.

Girls may take on queer little ways—put on mannerisms in speaking or dramatic ways of walking.

They may become very critical of their parents, even acting a little ashamed of them. Boys sometimes want to be left alone, not to be questioned about their affairs. A mother tells of going into her thirteen-year-old son's bedroom to say good night—the only reward she got was: "Mom, can't a fellow have any privacy in this house, even when he goes to bed?"

Adolescents are likely to become very sensitive about the things and rights that are personal—opening or reading mail addressed to them, going through their pockets or dresser drawers, reading their diaries, or criticizing their friends.

There is something about receiving a letter addressed "to me" that makes it strictly private in an adolescent's mind. And "Dear Diary" is almost like a friend or other self to which one can tell anything with perfect security. Finding that someone has tampered with letters of her very own or dared to break open the diary that holds her innermost thoughts is very hard for an adolescent girl to take.

A mother felt that the content of letters coming to her daughter was troubling her. Having a conscience on such matters she hesitated to read them even though they were left about freely, yet she felt she had to know what they contained. She debated the matter and then consulted me.

As we talked it over, it seemed best for her to raise the question of the letters' content without in any way suggesting there was any impropriety in her receiving them. If then she was not satisfied that all was well, she might say to the daughter that she felt she must see them but also say, "I know letters are very private. I could have read them but I felt I could not take such an advantage. Letters *are* personal. But I feel I must know about these. Will you give them to me or must I go and get them?"

Her fourteener said, "I never hid the letters because I trusted you."

Reporting the incident the mother said, "When she told me that, I was so happy I had not read these letters without her knowledge!" The daughter went on to explain that she had wanted to tell her mother what was in the letters, *but "I didn't know what you would do!"* It happened the letters were from a former schoolmate now moved away. She feared she was pregnant and had written to ask whether the boy with whom she had gone before moving was now going with anyone else.

Mother and daughter talked over this situation and together decided on a plan to help the unfortunate girl who had written the letters. This mother did not embarrass her teen-age daughter. And the daughter found that sharing the letters was a relief.

Albert wrote rather nice poetry. But his mother never knew he even had poetic thoughts until one day, while cleaning his room, she came upon a diary with several poems he had written. Naturally she was proud of them. Shortly afterward she read several of them to a group she had in the home. No one present knew that Albert had returned home during the reading; his mother carefully replaced the diary in his room where she had found it.

A few days later she eagerly looked in the precious little book for more of Albert's verse. Alas, there was no more added! So she asked him about it. He went upstairs to his room, came down at once, handed the diary to his mother, and said, "Here, Mother, take it. It's no longer *my* book!" Morbid? Yes. But that little volume was very much privately his own.

When our adolescent children seem unreasonably resentful about what seems to us is our rightful interest in them, when they complain that we can't let them have any privacy, that we criticize their friends unduly, that we pry into their affairs, we would be less hurt if we understand that this *resentment is not directed specifically toward us as persons.*

No, it is merely that our children are outreaching for adequacy. *And that we,* being their parents and so right in their area of living day by day, *get in their way!* Of necessity. Yes, of necessity—because they are not yet sufficiently grown up to manage all their affairs of living. But we can't blame them for trying to do just that. It is hard for us as parents to admit—and harder "to take" day by day—but a contentious thirteen-year-old may be a much more promising candidate for adequate adulthood than a sweet, yielding child.

As our early teeners develop new and different phases, a good thing to remember is: "This, too, shall pass." It isn't always easy to work along inch by inch—praising, criticizing, giving free permissions and emphatic "Noes" in the right places. Though they try to argue with us as though they are already adult, we must never make the mistake of trying to meet them as on the childish level. We must always be the mature adults in the situation, for *no home can stand two generations of adolescents at the same time.*

While the early teen-ager has to make adjustment to the physical changes that beset him—pimples on the face, the large nose, becoming "too tall," lagging behind and being called "the runt," blushing easily, sometimes sputtering in speech, worried over complexion or oiliness of hair—he needs the *warmth of understanding* all about him. If he has to manage his own emotions and those of his parents also, that creates a greater strain than he is usually able to take.

In counseling with these early teeners, I find one of their major conflicts is with their parents. Many of these conflicts are in the normal program of growing up; they cannot be avoided. The problem is to keep them from becoming too intense lest the possible good influence of the parents be lost and the children seek ways to avoid their parents and to deceive them. Unless the early adolescent finds understanding at home he is likely to become evasive, and then parents find themselves unable to help as they so much desire to do.

Maturity and stability at home—these help adolescents to develop the habit of feeling secure anywhere. Mothers who cry overmuch, fathers who lose their tempers habitually, conflict between parents—these are problems distressed adolescents bring to me. If the boy and girl can know that Dad and Mom are together in this business of living at home, that Dad will hold his temper and Mom control her emotions until they can all see things straight together, well, *they feel secure,* safe.

I feel almost helpless when Jane says, "I can't talk anything over with my mother; she just goes all to pieces, scolds or cries." Or when Bill explains, "No use to try to talk to Dad. He'll just get mad and tell me off." Perhaps I ask Tim, "Have you talked this over with your Dad?" He may say, "No use; he'll close up like a clam."

Now I know that one reason some parents give such responses to their adolescent children is that they feel at a loss to know how to help. But the fact is that when early teen-agers find such reactions at home, they feel lost, inadequate, sometimes even desperate. The outside world of early teen-agers with others of their kind is so uncertain that they need desperately to feel that at home things are settled and stable.

One of the first questions an early teener asks about an adult is: "Is he fair to me?" He knows instinctively that his parents, his teachers, have the advantage. He needs to be convinced that his parents in particular will not use their advantage against him.

A lad in a Chicago group asked, "Why do our folks laugh at us about serious things?"

"What do you have on your mind?" I asked.

"Well," he responded, "I'm fifteen. I like a girl. I know we'll never marry; but what I feel for her is pretty fine. Dad just laughs and says, 'Puppy love stuff.' I don't see why Dad can't understand that as a fifteen-year-old kid I can have fine feelings toward a girl."

Probably the father hadn't the slightest idea he was humiliating his growing-up son. But he might have talked to the son about the first girl *he* liked. That would have created a bond of union between them, mutual understanding.

Our early teeners resent very keenly their parents using their discipline advantages in the presence of others. They know they must be disciplined; but they are deeply humiliated when it is done before an audience. In a crisis this may sometimes be necessary; then it must be done. But as a rule, discipline should be in private.

One early January morning as our train was nearing its destination, we were sitting before the mirror in the ladies dressing room—she a vivid fourteen-year-old combing her beautiful blonde tresses, I arranging my graying hair. She was so very grown-up. I could almost feel her reaching out for the measurement of her own dignity! She talked of the Christmas holiday at her grandmother's, of her school's opening the next Monday morning—*then Mother entered.* She fixed her accusing eyes on my growing-up companion and with maternal discipline accused: "Patty, you never returned my tooth paste I loaned you last night."

In a very grown-up but very respectful voice my growing-up companion replied, "Well, Mother, I thought I could give it to you this morning."

The mother took the proffered tube of paste and

continued, "You should learn to return things, Patty. I wanted it earlier this morning."

Patty looked at her mother with something in her eyes akin to hate. She hastily finished her hair, her pride crumbled—and no more conversation!

Now Patty should have returned the borrowed tooth paste. She had inconvenienced her mother. Granted all that. But what had the mother done to Patty? She had humiliated her in a situation she was managing with a grownup—an experience that made her feel herself grown-up, capable, adequate. Was the point the mother made worth what it cost Patty? Nice question. It is possible that her humiliation was the thing Patty would remember rather than the lesson that she should promptly return all borrowed articles.

It isn't always easy to choose the right moment, I know. Parents are busy, and "right now while I feel like it" is a pretty strong urge. We've had our Pattys through a good deal of immaturity. Didn't we "turn her up" and spank her when she disobeyed? Haven't we said, "Now, Patty, Mother wants you to stop that this very minute," perhaps when she was reaching for some breakable object with her unsteady childish hands? How many times we said to *little* Patty, "Now, Patty, if you do that again, I'll punish you!"

How very hard to see that now the once-little Patty is growing up, feels very much a person on her own. And that she cares dreadfully about her dignity. Not little Patty of seven years ago or even of a year ago, but now a Patty with a sense of separateness and demanding that she be treated not like a child but like another person.

There come times when parents must be emphatic and relentless in their demands upon their children; but there must also be deep fellowship and understanding between them. Some things parents may wisely ignore; other things simply cannot be passed by. The mother needs to keep persistently after her daughter as to certain household responsibilities. Many things the daughter wishes to do that she must not be allowed to do.

For instance, there is now much of too early dating. The mother needs to be adamant about late nights and about going places for which the daughter is not sufficiently mature to manage whatever situation might develop in such places. About such matters the daughter needs to feel the finality of the mother's decisions. Dad will need to be equally final about some of Junior's responsibilities. Driving the car, late nights, drinking—these illustrate.

But along with these finalities there may and should be fellowship and appreciation—points on which parents and children agree and in which they work happily together.

Children do not truly respect parents who are afraid to say, "No!" As a boy in Atlanta put it, "Sometimes our parents are softies—they're scared to tell us off." And these early teeners can take straight talk *if they feel it is fair* and that we understand *how they feel* about things. They dislike peevishness, bickering, cowardice, bullying. They do respect fairness, good sportsmanship, and frankness—above all, *frankness.* For they instinctively know that frankness is a compliment to themselves. They seldom will tell you they like it, but they do!

Parents are such necessary nuisances to early teeners! They must have great humility, almost impossible patience, and all but superhuman understanding to live with their early teen-agers without hurting them irreparably or getting hurt and broken themselves. *To be a really good parent is Godlike indeed!* It is to have the understanding experience brings yet never to ridicule inexperience in those who are ours. It means to discipline without taking advantage of our superior power. It means to heal the hurts of failure with guidance toward the right way. It means to love beyond what we have any right to expect our children can understand or appreciate.

Being a good parent means being so like God that it is impossible to be one without knowing him. And the best fellowship of parents and children is that in which both feel—each for himself and in his own way—the *redeeming security* found only in that One who is the Parent of all believers.

II

OUR EARLY-TEENERS AWAY FROM HOME

"It's ten o'clock—I wonder where that child can be?" How many times Dad has heard Mother's anxious voice asking this question. Perhaps it's Patricia; or it may be Bill. No matter which, when you ask such questions you think longingly of the time past when you gathered them around the table or tucked them in at night. But now those days are over.

Instead of the children Patricia and Bill once were, you have persons living in your home who must have outside contacts. At least they feel they must have these outside-the-home contacts. And deep down you know also that they must have them if they are to grow up normally. But even while you are trying to get used to these new persons and their new needs, your Bill seems so sure he has ideas that are superior to yours, and your Patricia looks at you pityingly and wonders how you can be so old-fashioned about what *nice* girls can do *these* days.

Parents of early teeners have the delicate job of balancing the time their children need to be at home with what time they are to spend on outside contacts. There is also the question of deciding how their time will be spent both at home and away. And this involves the problem of what the outside contacts are to be. It's not an easy balance to strike.

Being "too strict" is not the way; "turning them loose" is dangerous. Sometimes parents make the mistake of shifting from one extreme to the other. This breaks down the respect of the child for the parent. Here as in other things children have the right to grow up feeling *they can depend on their parents.* Parents who discipline themselves to be steady toward their growing-up children will find at once that they can be steady only when they are reasonable and sound in disciplining their children.

Bill and Patricia, if all has gone well until now, have felt a real sense of family responsibility as children. But right now in the earlier teens they will normally be much more conscious of their love for outside activities. It may seem for a time that their anxiety to get away from home most of the time has actually eclipsed all the home responsibility they had earlier developed. Parents may be hurt deeply by what they see of this on the surface.

It will relieve the hurt if we realize that all this is a passing phase of growing up into the sort of persons who can get along without us as active, directing, and supporting parents. Children who never become sufficiently mature to do without parents can seldom do much for themselves—or, what may be more important, much for their own children later.

A mother was stunned when her fourteen-year-old daughter said to her, "Mother, you just *must* know that it makes more difference to me what the kids think of me than what you and Dad think!"

"How *can* she say that? We gave her life; we have given her every opportunity; no one can care for her as we do!" said the mother. She was brokenhearted.

Dad was all for putting their daughter "in her place."

"How can she turn against us?" asked Mother in despair.

But that wasn't what their daughter was doing. She had no way of knowing how cruel it was to say this thing to her mother; she couldn't possibly understand that it wasn't altogether true. She understood only that she had a world to make outside her home. And *right then* it seemed that Dad and Mom were hindering her from making this world of *hers*.

It takes wise parents to so guide their children in building this outside world that they feel home is helping them to do it. For our children up to now have had little experience in using moral judgment in situations outside their homes. Their intense eagerness to be with others, to belong, to be thought well of by others besides their families is likely to lead them into trouble unless they have skilful guidance from their parents. This is especially important for children from Christian homes.

No matter how carefully the atmosphere of the home has been kept true to the Christian essentials, the moment children step outside it for their friends and associates and social activities, that moment they are surrounded by many things that are in direct conflict with all that Christian homes stand for.

In a sense these early teen years are the parents' last chance to give direct and compulsory guidance to their children in their outside relationships. These are the years when growing-into-mature-persons need the most help at this point. And fortunately most children with wise parents are, in their quieter moments with parents, willing to take suggestions that *seem to help them* in building a satisfactory outside world of their own.

Wise parents will always be on the alert to discuss with their early teeners ways to make good and satisfying and happy contacts outside the home—especially Christian parents! For there will of necessity be so many points on which they will be compelled to say an emphatic "No." If these positive denials are balanced with satisfying guidance toward constructive experiences, the ordinary early teener has a much better chance of coming through these difficult years in a way to make both him and his parents happy as they look back upon them.

Clothes seem very important to early teen girls. Things and skills to share become of tremendous importance to boys in these years. Why? Simply because they feel these things recommend them to groups outside their family circle.

Bill likes to show his football, his collection of stamps, his 4-H calf, his radio, something he made in manual training class. What he can do in the broad jump, how he can beat the drum or play the horn—all these help him to make easy and natural and satisfying contacts with groups. And so with Patricia in any of the things her parents can help her toward doing. Not as a finished adult skill—oh, no. But sufficiently well for her age that her contribution is accepted in her groups!

"Do people like me?" This is a question which haunts an early teener. He literally aches to belong. In fact he must belong if he is to mature into a real person. Sometimes his very eagerness may keep him from belonging; for with his inexperience he may use tactics that keep him from getting into the good graces of groups. He will seldom acknowledge such a failure. More often he will try to lay the blame on someone else.

"My folks will not let me do the things that would make me popular."

"My folks are too strict."

"My teacher has it in for me."

"Bill is jealous of me."

Other times when early teeners discuss their social failures with an older person, they may explain by saying the reason is something they cannot overcome.

"I'm a runt and so can't play football."

"I'm not pretty like Jane who thinks she's so smart."

"I don't live in a nice house like the rest of the kids."

"My mother won't let me do what all the other kids do."

Sometimes early teeners develop great sensitivity about going places with their parents or even about appearing in school functions where their parents are present. One mother who was her high school

P.T.A. president said her daughter told her she didn't want her to sit on the platform at the assembly when the P.T.A. was presenting a speaker.

"That hurt," said the mother. "I should think she would be proud."

The daughter was a very sensitive fourteen-year-old girl not doing too well in her studies. She was so self-conscious over this that having her mother on the platform seemed to highlight her own mediocre achievement rather than giving her a sense of pride.

When parents go out socially with their early teeners, they should take great care to be well groomed and not to do anything that might embarrass their children. Especially should they try to observe the customs of the occasion—what their children have observed that "everybody is expected to do."

Our early teeners cannot build the best possible social world for themselves without the help of parents. Other adults may help them, of course. But the younger adolescent can better endure the social rebuffs from his own group he is bound to get, if he knows his parents are standing by ready to help. Early teeners are sometimes terribly cruel to each other. When one of them gets hurt by this sort of psychological cruelty, nothing can take the place of parents whom the child has learned he can trust to talk over all such things and to help and encourage him.

It's the two-sidedness of these early teen years that tests parents' insight and skill. Here is Jim—"such a big boy!" And here's Mary Ann—"taller than her mother!" Their parents, moving out from their own inner stability and emotional poise and religious faith, must treat this not-yet-man and this not-yet-woman without suggesting the "not-yet" part of it all—must treat them according to their height, shall we say? Yet their parents must never forget the inexperience-with-the-world, the over-eagerness for outside approvals.

And when discussion is not enough, then their own greater experience in their own practiced skills in rating social approvals must come into play and be used for their children's advantage. If this means saying, "No," then it should be said firmly and finally—and the Jims and Mary Anns should know by experience that the word means exactly "No" and nothing else.

In a general way the physical experience of adolescence is somewhat the same in all who pass from childhood to adulthood; but individuals may differ much in their emotional reactions while the process goes on. This may show in the way they get along—or fail to get along—with their schoolmates or with their groups. All parents naturally wish their Bill and Marge would walk off with every group honor and have all their crowd feeling they couldn't get along without them. Or should we say that most parents may be tempted to wish for something like that? But it seldom happens that way.

Some time ago a mother came to me about her fourteen-year-old daughter. "Mary is so terribly unhappy," she explained. I asked her why. "She is never socially included," replied the mother. "She is never invited to parties or asked to belong to clubs." I could see at once that this had been a great disappointment to the mother.

When I talked with Mary she said exactly that. "I have disappointed Mother. I do bring home good grades; but Mother thinks I should be the most popular of them all and I'm just not." I found this girl was of a very sensitive type. She would find it very difficult to take a social rebuff. If she received one, her first and natural reaction would be to withdraw from her own age group and to seek the protection of an encouraging adult until her morale was rebuilt so that she could seek other social contacts. Mary did exactly this—and she paid her mother the compliment of talking with her rather than with anyone else at first.

Her mother merely blamed her for not being more socially successful. So Mary had a second rebuff—and where it really hurt. So she withdrew from her mother also. The withdrawal from her age group might be remedied—the withdrawal from her mother was something much more serious.

It may be that Mary will never be the social success that her mother wishes she might be. But I could see at once that she had the capacity to become a charming and delightful social creature. She was rightfully entitled *as her mother's child* to get help from her mother rather than the sharp hurt of being accused of failure. What the mother did would have been very poor teaching—it was even worse "parenting."

She might have put herself on Mary's side—helped

her to understand the "why" of that particular social failure with her outside group—talked over ways of avoiding such failures in the future—perhaps even found a way to overcome this unfortunate experience. Then she might have shared with Mary as she went on to succeed. And that would have bound Mary to her.

I see too much of this *pushing of young girls to be popular.* Often Mother minds it all more than the daughters. And Mother's paraded unhappiness over it makes the daughters feel failures when they are merely being their own selves—often not genuine social failures at all but merely not following the much-more-mature pattern of social life which the experienced mother demands.

A father and mother came to talk about their thirteen-year-old Jim who didn't seem able to get along well with groups of his own age. Jim was a very aggressive person—*so was his father.* And Jim admired his father greatly! The son was boastful, something of an exhibitionist. Naturally other boys in his age group retaliated—tried to "put him in his place." Word got to the father and mother. Dad lectured him; Mom worried over him. They feared they had on their hands a son doomed to failure throughout life because he wasn't successful in his group contacts now. Had Jim been eighteen instead of thirteen, they might indeed have been concerned. But he was only thirteen. For him—as for all early teeners—there was still time to learn better techniques.

Said Jim's dad, "What worries me most is that,

along with the way he feels hurt over his trouble with other boys, he seems also rather to enjoy the fights he gets into." That was just it. He did enjoy his scrapping *somewhat.* It dramatized him; he was the cause of something exciting. In his inexperience he didn't understand that getting along with others is more satisfying than fighting with them. He was simply growing up and trying out the people and groups around him. And all without any adult reasoning about it. It simply came naturally to him.

The more his mother worried, the more excited his father became each time he lectured Jim; and that made it all the more exciting for the son, more dramatic. Jim was bright, he had abounding energy. His age group seemed entirely too tame. Therefore he felt unconsciously that he must do something to cause excitement. Not that Jim ever sat down and figured this all through for himself. No, he merely found outlet in these ways for some of his energy and his *simple desire to be active about something,* to be in the center of something.

It is thought by many that much delinquency has its roots in something like this. Dad and Mom can do a great deal to keep such a lad *challenged,* busy developing some talent he has so that he has opportunities to do things before others and so get recognition satisfactions.

Such a boy who is aggressive by nature will always have the urge to be a leader. This will get him into some of the troubles that always beset leaders, of course. His dad can share with him some of his own early teen experiences, some of the wallops he got. When such an aggressive lad gets into trouble of the *ordinary* sort, it is better that the parents do not run to help him out by putting things straight for him. Much better to help him in the home to see ways he can straighten out his own difficulties.

Then there is the early teener who makes his social contacts easily and maintains them without any special difficulty. Often he may stay with his groups too long. Or he may be so desirous of keeping his friends that he cannot say, "No." Or he may simply be a "natural" for social living.

Early teeners of all of these types desire to be socially accepted. In some there are more serious conflicts within—conflicts between the various desires, for example. The experience of conversion includes the conflict between the merely human desires and the desire for all that mature Christians include in their understanding of the redeemed life. This experience resolves the conflict so that relaxation takes its place. Instead of "fightings within" there comes satisfaction with what is to be found in "the higher life."

Early teeners will differ also in their adjustments to groups outside their families. Some will find their group places readily, in church or school or community organization. Others will require more time and effort before they feel at home with such groups as are open to them at their age.

The understanding parent knows that the early teen years are a period for learning some of the first and some of the most important lessons about association with the outside world of persons and groups. And the parent who is mature also will hold steady and keep helpful while he guides his early teen offspring into his own rightful adequacy. He will supply for the time and so far as he can that adequacy, that dependability, that ongoingness which he prays his child may finally know fully in his own mature experience of God.

Many times I have had to go to mothers with the unfortunate experiences of their daughters. I remember now the mother who looked at her daughter who really needed her terribly and exclaimed, "To think you would bring this disgrace on me?" She wept because *she* was hurt rather than for the hurt of her child. Her own hurt pride seemed more important than *help for the daughter.*

But I remember another mother who put her arms around the daughter instantly—her daughter came first, you see. Then she turned to me and said, "Thank you, lady, for what you have done." And then—words of supreme parental *devotion* and *wisdom of technique*—"I want you to know *she has a family.*" That kind of mother can kneel with her daughter before God's mercy seat and help her to experience God's healing redemption.

"Mom, all the other kids do it!"

"I'm the only one who has to get in by ten o'clock."

"All the other girls date when they're fourteen."

"All the other fellows can drive a car."

"Dad, you must remember I'm no longer a baby."

"I'll bet you did these things when you were my age."

Do these phrases have a familiar sound to your parental ears? They do if there are early teeners in your house. And here are some of the places parents must learn to say "No" so that it is understood throughout the household that "That's that!" Only —and this is so very important—it is easier to put down the parental foot finally and emphatically if that foot has already taken a good many steps along the way *with* the boy and girl, and also if that voice has already shown it can help in the things both parents and children want to do. Help on things they *may* do—good things, wholesome things, constructive things—this is the best way to prepare for that inevitable time when the parents' united maturity must save boys and girls in the home from making mistakes by doing outside what they are entirely too immature to attempt safely.

She seemed utterly broken as she sat before me, this good, hardworking mother, and related her story in tones of infinite sadness. "It seems my thirteen-year-old Rachel and I never say a kind word to each other." So I asked what seemed to be causing the most difficulty between them. "Dating," she said. "Rachel is too young to go out on dates."

How right this mother was—Rachel was too young to go out on dates. So her mother needed to hold steady emotionally. And to find where there was boy-and-girl group life in her community in which her Rachel might have good times with both boys and girls included. Rachel's mother needs to see if her church provides opportunity for group life with boys and girls together.

She must say, "No!" Of course. But that's not enough. She should be just as eager and emphatic in seeing that outside her home in the community, in the school, in the church there is provided group social life where Rachel can have good times safely until she has reached the maturity and experience that will enable her to date with greater safety.

Everywhere I go the question of late nights comes up. These early teeners need about ten hours of sleep. Parents are to blame for late nights. If the parents were to say, "Our early teeners have to be home at an early hour," school and community projects would have to conform. I know some parents who are doing exactly that.

In every community there are questionable places. Regardless of who goes to them, parents who are wise see to it that their children do not go there. But here again it is not enough to keep children in their early teens from such places. Other places must be provided where they can go with Christian propriety.

Even Jesus shocked and grieved his mother when he had to find outside his home ways to serve his Father: "Wist ye not that I must be about my Father's business?" Parents naturally feel hurt when they discover that their children can no longer find under the parental roof all the opportunities they need in order to grow up. And how naturally parents wish they might keep them little boys and girls. But in them is the spark God put there—to grow, to experience, to create on their own. And the love of Christian parents should be redemptive—redeeming the process from what is unworthy and saving it for all the possible good outcomes.

Christian parents are successful when their children not only do as Dad and Mom say but come in their own way to the place where they say with a deep sense of faith, "Lord, I believe." And "Take my life and let it be consecrated, Lord, to Thee." We cannot always dominate our children's lives; but we can introduce them to the *compelling* love of God.

Our early teeners—as they find their way outside their childhood homes—need to be understood, to be guided, to be denied harmful experiences, to be exposed to rich and exhilarating and creative experiences as they are growing up toward their fulfilment of life. Parents' righteousness should not alienate children—it should win them.

III

AT HOME WITH OUR MIDDLE-TEENERS

"She is so grown-up she really frightens me sometimes," confided a mother to me this very day. She was speaking of her fifteen- ("near sixteen-") year-old daughter, Joan. This mother continued, "Sometimes she seems as old as I am."

Joan is now perhaps as tall as she will ever be. She no longer fumbles with her hands. Her voice has taken on that richness and steadiness of more adult life. The ungainly bodily awkwardness of yesteryear has given way to good general symmetry. Her physical development has emerged with definite form to give the finishing touch of genuine feminine attractiveness. Joan *is* a young lady.

Bill—the boy in whom she's been interested, although she had thought he "was too short for her" —has in these last few months passed her in height. There has been a marked increase in his general vigor. Along with this increase in physical vigor, vocal changes are going on—from the thin treble of boyhood to an octave below. Sometimes he uses both in speaking one word. Hair begins to grow on his face. His hips begin to thin; his shoulders and chest begin to grow broader; his chest may flatten somewhat. Bill *is* physically a man.

Joan's definiteness as a woman has been established. Joan is no longer *physically* becoming a woman—her glandular balance has achieved womanhood. There is a reason why Joan seems more grown-up—she *is* a woman.

Bill is just as definitely a man.

Both are now definitely developed as man and woman. Between them there is a definite separateness. They are physically different. Bill has developed the capacity to become a father, Joan that to become a mother. They each have distinct functions to perform. *They are a new and normal challenge to each other.* And this fundamental separateness and challenge must be understood and appreciated by parents and, indeed, by all adults who would deal wisely with the Bills and Joans.

In a primitive yarn there is the account of Big Tooth and the Swift One—and of the wooing flight of Big Tooth for the Swift One when they had come to this period of development. According to the tale, the two first built a shelter in a tree, then later a permanent dwelling as had their ancestors. It sounds *so* simple. The parents of Big Tooth and the Swift One felt no need to plan for that social and mental and spiritual maturing which would give direction to their physical maturity.

At physical maturity came mating and offspring. Each generation lived out its days on the same level as its parents had done. A simple sort of existence, yes. But it would satisfy neither Christian parents nor their children in this less simple culture of our day.

Yet the tale may help us to appreciate the conflict

in which our senior high school boys and girls find themselves. There are the normal physical urges; there are the proper demands of a Christian civilization that mating be put off for a time until Bill and Joan have had time to understand better what marriage and parenthood mean.

If parents could look upon their middle-teeners, think of them as having almost fully developed bodies, understand the difference this makes to their children, and then purposefully develop fellowship with these *physically mature* personalities in their households, they could help greatly in sustaining and holding them steady, clean, and fine while they go on to mature their personalities. The developed body with the immature capacity for its control and direction—here is the source of the most serious problems parents have in dealing with their middle-teeners.

It is "for such a time as this" that parents have had all their own opportunities for building highly developed personalities and skills of fellowship—this time with its swiftly passing days of opportunities for maturing fellowship with children-becoming-persons-on-their-own.

As middle-teeners sense their own definiteness of person, they are likely to exhibit more definite temperaments and ideas and attitudes. They may want to spend more time alone. The girl's own room becomes a haven to her, and her possessions seem more personal. She may have many thoughts she does not care to share with the rest of the family. In fact, all things pertaining to her are of great importance. She is, probably unconsciously, seeking to create a definite and unique setting which befits her new sense of unique and separate selfhood.

Her eating, the table settings, the fitness of her surroundings—in fact, each item in the settings where she sees herself becomes of new and special importance to her. She may develop snobbishness. Or if of intense temperament, she may even come to have a fixed expression of disgust and contempt—the tilted head, the dilated nostrils, the downward look toward all but her own special group, the quizzical look which seems to say, "*You* have been weighed in the balances and found wanting!"

Such are some of the passing phases. Artificial she may seem, not because she is mean or shallow, but because she is *inexperienced* in managing her new sense of separateness.

As for boys during these years, our Jim may become very critical. He may take flights into day-dreaming, sometimes seeming far away from what is going on around him. He may be moody—one moment being most unusually tender and protective and the next starting out to conquer the world with his own two bare hands.

Both boys and girls may become highly secretive and selective about friends and their own affairs. When they bring their friends home, they want to be left alone with them. They resent terribly your "looking their friends over." They may at times be very argumentative, wanting to argue every little point. Or they may be "smooth," accepting anything and everything, leaving you quite baffled as you wonder what they really are thinking.

Middle-teeners are quite likely to be investigative. Sometimes they seem perfectly uncanny in the way they find out things. They may seem to take special delight in finding you in the wrong about some statement you have made or something you have done and then "play it for all it is worth."

"Now, *Mother*" sometimes sounds almost paternal and tempts Mother to feel foolish or defensive. When Junior with an almost coddling voice says, "No-o-o-w, Dad!" Dad looks at his "young whippersnapper" of a son and, well, he *doesn't* like it. But Junior is having *such* a wonderful time.

The desire to break things open—to see what makes them tick—they express toward persons as well as things. It often leads them in certain definite directions in their interests and activities. Parents may see it working out in their children's schoolwork, in the friends they select, in their reading, in their social life. So this is the time they should have an abundance of opportunities to enter into many experiences, for these experiences will challenge whatever of capacity there is in them. The school play, the church choir, the band, the French club, the Sunday school class—such as these will furnish good and wholesome avenues for these naturally enterprising and investigative middle-teeners to push along.

The way they may give each new enterprise "everything they have" and how they leave off the former deep interests and take on new—both show the more physically mature body with its greater physical energy and nervous energy, the feeling of surging drives to do things, and at the same time the still immature capacity that later selects a vocation and a limited round of other interests and then sticks to them more or less persistently. The wise parent will sympathize constructively in both the intensity and the brevity of many of the activities of their offspring at this time. And such parents will be undisturbed by either.

Gathering lasting mementoes of occasions that would otherwise be merely memories shows personality development in these middle-teen years. Newly significant now are the place card, the especially nice paper napkin with many names written on it, pennants on the wall, trophies won, the autograph collection. Meeting significant people begins to count. "Just fooling around" is not nearly so interesting as it was a short year ago.

Now these growing personalities like not only to see *something going on*; they like to see something shaping up, something changing, something growing into something else, the personally dramatic rather than still life.

John had always gone with his parents on their vacation and had always seemed to like driving through the country seeing "this and that." But having reached sixteen, he hurt them one day by declaring, "I don't want to go with Dad and you this year."

"Why ever not?" exclaimed his mother.

"Oh, it's no fun just to drive around and look—I'd get bored."

But when—wise parents as they were!—they included in the plan a national league game and visits to several of the country's largest stadia, John was all agog. These items tied in with his regular interests. *But* he then wanted to take along one of his friends. So they slept in cabins and tourist homes in order to make the vacation funds cover the friend's expenses also rather than stopping at hotels as originally planned.

"It was good for Dad and me; we learned that because John was growing-up, we never again *could* have him all to ourselves." Thus the mother spoke. Then she laughed—"Of course we missed those good beds and the good hotels."

"But," so she mused, "we can have all that when our John is struggling with his own John II."

Perhaps another year John will not care to go along with his parents for the vacation trip even with a friend. By the time he is eighteen, he will have separate plans for his own vacation. It may be that Dad and Mother have *had* their precious times—vacation times—with John. How good it will be to remember them as they watch their man-son make his own plans. And his plans should be better plans because of the fine times they have had together.

One of the big jobs of parents with their middle-teeners is to keep enough things going at home in which their children may find self-satisfaction. I know a family that is redecorating their home and doing all the work themselves. They are studying the better magazines on the subject. Another family is landscaping its yards, making pilgrimages to the woods to gather material. Perhaps a dutch oven can be built on the home yards; the house may need painting. Something in which ideas as well as work count—and in which all the family can co-operate.

Too bad if our middle-teeners ever think of home as "a place to eat and sleep and get away from as fast as I can, so there won't be a fight with Dad and Mother get to bawling" as one unfortunate sixteen-year-old said to me of his own home. For in a way these mid-teen years are the "swan song" of parents' chance with their children at home. They should be rich with all that Christian character in the parents can supply.

The self-assertion and self-display of our middle-teeners is more purposeful than when they were thirteen. Thus the giggling or tears of a thirteen-year-old girl are usually evidence merely of pent-up feeling. The two may come together or be separate; either way the activity gives release. But when a sixteen-year-old or a seventeen-year-old has crying spells, that calls for special attention and question as to the reason. Perhaps she feels helpless and uses crying to summon help.

If in her earlier years she has used the cudgel of self-pity and has gotten what she wanted by tears, her crying may seem a ready weapon and it may persist all of her life. Or if she has had the example of "crying-spells" set before her in the home, she may come unwittingly to use it as a sort of "social blackmail" to get what she thinks she wants. The tantrum has no normal place as a social method in the life of a healthy mid-teener.

Some time ago I was asked to counsel a boy of sixteen about his tantrums. When things did not go as he wanted or when he was crossed in any way, he would stalk out of class or committee meeting. If there was a door he could slam, he never missed the opportunity. A bright boy, he was thoroughly ashamed of these outbursts but he seemed unable to stop them. He couldn't explain why he put on such exhibitions.

As we conversed, it was revealed that he had a very "nervous" mother. His father, because he could never meet things forthrightly with his wife, became very domineering with his children. As this lad came to the period of development when he wanted to be self-assertive, he was frustrated, stopped, blocked.

His tantrums were not normal nor were they a carry-over of his younger teen habits. He strode out of meetings and slammed doors to make up for not having normal outlets for his natural feelings of self-assertion. The father was helped to see how he might remedy this by being less domineering and more companionable with this otherwise promising son of his.

Such a sad sixteen-year-old girl she was—pretty, bright, and unhappy with little self-confidence. She couldn't recite in class and enjoyed "running herself down." The girl was really self-abased and dejected.

She made good grades when they depended on written work. There was none of that youthful sparkle!

I learned that her mother was a socially aggressive woman, popular in social groups, and that her fourteen-year-old sister was much like the mother. It seemed rather useless for her to compete with a sparkling mother and sister for attention—so *why try?* She began to withdraw from groups, to *sit* and watch her mother and sister *in action.* She began to lose confidence in herself. But she had to feel some intensity about self; hence self-pity, self-abasement, dejection.

An extreme case, this girl illustrates how easy it is for a mid-teener to lose self-confidence. But *self-confidence is something the mid-teener must have!* He might better have too much than to have none.

Often the mid-teener is very lonely. He feels this increasingly separate existence from his family and yet he may not yet know how to establish himself in a social setting of his own. A lonely boy or girl is much more likely to "fall in love" and become serious about it than one who has parents who understand these in-between years and set up good fellowship with their children then.

Soon vocation, and a little later marriage, will serve to set up the new social system in which the developing personality will find itself supported. But for now nothing can take the place of good comradeship with parents in a permanent and lively family situation in giving the mid-teener the feeling he is supported, not alone, part of a going concern, *with* those who understand.

One time I was riding down a country road with a very fine friend. Said she, "This road is really quite precious to me. When I was sixteen I would feel so lonely. The supper dishes done, I felt I had to get away from the rest of the family. I would walk this half mile, *come back a person,* go up to my room to bed *content.*"

Thus in the midst of all the pressing and important *family* matters, these family matters after sixteen are less likely to be at the top of the list for attention. And the parents who try hardest to understand their children then must sometimes be hurt over the *separateness of interest* they see developing and reaching out from the family encirclement.

But although the developing sense of separateness may seem at times to put the parents in a sort of "all-give and no-get situation," this is usually far from the entire picture in parent-child relations at this stage of progress toward full personality. Merely seeing growth to keener appreciation, to greater sensitivity concerning values, and to enlarged capacity for loyalty and ideals can be most rewarding to any parent.

A new sense of tenderness often emerges here, and wise parents can share in this. One might call it *romanticising* life. A boy is likely to find a girl he feels is "The One." A girl may feel a fine sense of loyalty to a particular boy. Parents are wise who work along with this rather than driving their children into love affairs by being critical toward the outside member of such associations and thus making their own child feel he (or she) must protect the admired or loved one against the unfairness of his own parents.

There came the time when one mother felt she should say to her sixteen-year-old son, "Tom, I know she's *wonderful!* But I want her to be happy as well as you. And you are both a little too young to get serious yet, aren't you?"

And Tom looked to his mother and responded, "Gee, Mom, you're swell. I guess though you're right about this."

His mother had *appreciated his adored.* Not long after he reported, "Mom, I guess you *were* right. I'm going with another girl, Rose; and she's just as nice as Jane was—maybe a little nicer." How all but fatal to good mother-son fellowship it would have been for this mother to have put herself *between* Tom and Jane!

But this distinctly personal phase of appreciation and devotion, this growth in personal tenderness, goes hand in hand with increased sensitivity to religious experience and truly spiritual values. Christian parents will go along with their mid-teeners in these also. They will find ways to experience with their children great moments in worship, sharing with each other the refinements of feeling which such experiences bring.

An auto trip may include services in some church not usually available. Music in the home may readily include some of the most spiritually stirring and assuring. They are masters of the fine art of "parenting" who can share in such spiritual emotion with their children but never intrude on ground that seems sacred to their now-being-separated-from-home mid-teeners.

They are fortunate parents and offspring alike who learn during these years in such matters of spiritual appreciation and culture to use mere words the less and to employ moments of "unsaid" understanding the more. For the mutual understanding is the vital thing; words are merely its instrument, the means to bring it into being.

Here they are—our mid-teeners on the threshold of complete independence of their parental family. They feel increasing separateness, a compelling desire to be on their own, a getting ready to mate and to support their own family. Now it is their own career, their own love, their own family that are challenging. But we parents must support the "getting-ready"; we must do the stabilizing while they mature until they can manage their own affairs. We must help them through their periods of "lostness" and loneliness, through their frustrations and failures, their achievements and victories, so that they come through without bad habits or emotional quirks, able to be good and healthy-souled husbands, wives, parents.

Soon they are gone—to college, away at their first job, establishing their own homes. We want them to be sufficient for those things—self-reliant, fair, stable, unselfish. We want them to be better wives and husbands, and they *must* be better parents, than we have been.

IV

OUR MID-TEENERS AWAY FROM HOME

The seventeen-year-old girl dropped exhausted into the first available chair and exclaimed to her mother, "There are times when I envy you your easy time!" Said the mother as she reported this about her senior high school daughter, "I simply burst out laughing. I do my own work; there are four in the family. More than once I have looked at Sarah and thought to myself how carefree she was."

But as the girl began to name over the many things she had to do, the mere enumeration showed her daughter to her in a new light. Glee club, a senior party, a part in the senior play, an all-day Saturday job in a store to provide part of the money for graduation expenses, the nominating committee of the Girl's Friendly Society in her high school, all the activities of her Sunday school class and of the young people's group in her church—it was quite a recital! And this mother was honest enough to say, "I do have a more secure and easier life than my Sarah. She was right in what she said that day she came home so thoroughly worn out."

Our mid-teeners—fifteen to eighteen years old but still *our children!*—have a more complex world in which to live than has any other generation of American youth. It takes more to make good in their outside world, more moral understanding and courage simply to keep decent than you had to deliver when you were at that age.

The other night in a city of Georgia a group of high school students came up to chat after the public meeting was over and with them a few of the parents lingered also. Said the spokesman for the high school group, "I don't think our parents know our outside world. They really don't know how to be interested in it—it is so much different!" And these are some of the things different students said after a little questioning:

"We take courses in high school that our parents never had—psychology, for instance."

"We have to choose our activities more carefully than did they. There are so many more of them."

"We have keener competition everywhere than they had. We compete even to be accepted in college. The question used to be whether one could get the money to go; now we have to have the money and the brains as well."

"We have to grow up faster because we have so many decisions to make," and they began to enumerate. Decisions having to do with military training's effect on all of one's plans, for instance. Is it worth while to start college? Can one get in? Because of such considerations, should boys get married earlier than they otherwise would? And if boys cannot go through college in the regular way, girls wonder whether *they* should try to.

When this small group had finished, one of the parents said, "Our world is really not as complex as theirs." This is true whether you live in the open country, in a small village, in the county seat, or in a large city. This generation of mid-teeners have a hectic world and a turmoil of emotions to manage.

The other night a man arose in open forum and said, "All this talk about youth's world and life being different is exaggerated. Young people are just the same as they have always been; their life decisions are no more difficult than they have always been, no more so than when I was in my teens forty years ago."

I felt the teachers in that group simply gasp. Yet that man was so sincere. The response to what he had said was: "We walk by the same method we used a hundred or even a thousand years ago. But the problems of walking are much more numerous these days. Our habits of walking have changed therefore. It is now much more hazardous to walk; *it now takes more intelligence to walk and keep alive* than it did when you were a boy." For a moment the man looked beaten. But he was honest. Then he said such a fine thing: "I guess I've lost step because I have to walk more slowly than I used to."

So easy it is to lose step with youth! Could it be that this genuinely honest and good man chose to think of walking as it was when he was young merely because it was easier then for him to walk than it is now?

Parents must learn to thrust their understanding into youth's world as well as to know the way these mid-teeners feel at their stage of growing-up. Too many parents have "washed their hands" of their mid-teeners' outside world saying, "It's beyond me —I just give up!" Or perhaps they've proclaimed vehemently, "I didn't do any such thing when I was young, and you're not going to either!"

Such parents have not realized that to turn a mid-teener loose in his outside world means almost certain tragedy. Nor have they realized that demanding he follow exactly your youth patterns means that you break him, make him a hypocrite, or turn him into a defiant, maladjusted person. Being a good parent today takes *rare humility* as well as stamina and courage.

So often one hears, "Dad's a great guy, but he really doesn't know much about me." Or "Mother's all right. I think sometimes I hurt her awfully. I just don't seem to be able to help it!" When one appreciates that these parents literally ache to help their children and that these children feel so desperately their need of parental counsel, one is tortured to find a way to bring these parents and mid-teeners to a better understanding of each other.

Take the growing sense of separateness mid-teeners naturally and properly feel. They cannot feel helplessly bound to their parents any longer. Out there in their own future world they see their own jobs, their own mates, their own families. Trying to keep them bound to you is unkind; seeking to keep their respect and love is necessary to both them and yourselves. They have little time for your hurts, your disappointments, your health; their own present and future call for about all their time and thought.

Said one girl, "When my mother can't get me any other way, she can bring on a heart attack." It sounds so cruel! And the mother did have a nervous heart—it took only a little to start it beating too rapidly.

There was the lad who said to me, "My dad is sulking about something now. I'll have to wait until he gets over that before I can talk with him about this problem I have right now." In both cases these mid-teeners felt their parents were not sufficient for helping them with their problems. Their parents were demonstrating that they could not meet crises themselves.

We have confidence in our doctor, our pastor, our nurse—if they can help us through a crisis and thus help us toward our planning for the way through and out.

The thing that binds us to God is that we know he is able, that *always* "underneath are the everlasting arms!" Yes, and that even "though I walk through the valley of the shadow, Thou art with me."

The thing which sends a mid-teener to his parents in a crisis is that he knows they are adequate. He no longer comes to you as he once did merely because you are Dad and Mom and physically at hand. No, you must now be able to help him if he comes. As one girl put it concerning her own mother, "When I hear other girls talk about their mothers, I think mine must be pretty wonderful. She not only manages her own emotions but she helps me manage mine." And *this mid-teener just about said what parents are for.*

When parents project their interest into their children's outside world, they need to be careful lest they try to discover their own lost youth and thus overshadow their mid-teeners. Said a girl who was discussing her lack of happy social life, "I used to have gangs of the kids in but those times got to be Mother's parties. She simply walked off with everything." There is a difference between being a young person *with* young people and being an appreciative adult *entering in* with young people.

As a young college freshman girl so aptly put it one time, "I don't like kittenish women but I do like a good sport." When I asked her to tell what she meant by "kittenish" and "a good sport," she explained, "Kittenish women say symbolically and really, 'Come on, girls, let's all sit down on the floor and giggle together.' A good sport—well, a good sport acts her age but she doesn't get disgusted with me when I act mine." Our mid-teeners need happy, well-poised parents—personalities who are living and acting "their own age" and doing it successfully.

If we look honestly into the lives of our mid-teeners in the hope of understanding them, we shall see that they do have more maturing experiences of leadership than other generations have had.

I went into a high school of thirty-five hundred students. The principal introduced me to three young people—one was sixteen, the others seventeen. The sixteen-year-old presided. When he stood up he had sufficient "presence" that the great student body was quiet. The seventeen-year-old girl read the Scripture passage; she read so that her fellow students listened. The third student introduced me. No three highly-trained adults could have done all this more effectively.

Facing thirty-five hundred people is no small experience for anyone however skilled. And in almost all high schools there are many opportunities for maturing experiences. Consider athletics requiring physical co-ordination and also alert minds and controlled emotions. Think of what is involved in the finished productions of high school bands, their *á capella* choirs, their bands, their orchestras.

The other day I watched a Fourth of July parade. The work of the high school bands as they passed, their majorettes, the controlled marching of the musicians, the music they were producing—all about it was superior to what was being done by the American Legion band, by the fire departments, or by the various visiting community bands. Our mid-teeners are having multiple opportunities to develop leadership in doing things toward the finished manner.

With all this activity requiring control and poise, our mid-teeners are naturally advanced for their age in their social experiences and demands. And it is sad that they do not have the same specific skilled direction in their social life as they do in their school group activities.

School leaders rather expect parents to furnish training at this point. Actually mid-teeners are rather turned loose when it comes to questions of moral restraint. They certainly have fewer such restraints than did their parents at similar ages. They have greater freedom with the opposite sex. Dating habits have changed greatly. On every hand mid-teeners are sensitized to romance, and *nobody much* is giving a great deal of understanding help.

The mid-teen years have been called the "mating period" by many psychologists. So much is being said about "dating habits" in America today. There is much of taking courtship advantages when no courtship exists. There are a lot of "shoddy" courtships these days. Many boys and girls "pet" as a pastime—"neck" as a method of entertainment—rather than because they are in love with each other. And however much we may lament this, it is a folkway, a custom of the day. It is a *dangerous custom, a bad habit!*

Yes, the ways and habits of mate-seeking or dating or of courtship *have changed.* Your mid-teener sees these changed ways; he lives with them; they are a part of his world outside his own home. At the close of a workshop with parents lately, a mother came to me and said, "The other day my seventeen-year-old daughter hurt and surprised me terribly when I questioned her behavior with a youth."

"Oh, Mother," the daughter had remonstrated, "I don't think *you* have ever known how to be in love with anybody!"

"I had always thought," this mother went on,

"that Dad's and my life together must be a wonderful example to our children. Our courtship and marriage and all our family life had been *so* beautiful to us."

Now, of *course,* her daughter was expressing resentment at being questioned on what her mother had observed. But beyond all that, here was a mother who didn't quite see how very different is her daughter's courtship world. Nor had she fully appreciated how much more *dangerous* is that courtship world than her own had been. Her daughter perhaps actually feels scared and deep down has a feeling that something is wrong.

Adults are to blame for these precarious dating habits of youth. We have given very little training for our young people's dating in this complex world. We have not created situations in which there could be *good dating.* Boys no longer like to go to girls' homes for dates. Many parents have lost the genius for having boys and girls together in their homes.

Too many mid-teeners have too few opportunities at church for dating. Some time ago I addressed a Sunday night mid-teeners meeting—a senior high school group. I was pleased to see a number of couples, more than is at all usual. After the meeting more couples paired off. And when I looked out over my audience in the service which followed upstairs, I was happy again to see so many of those same couples sitting together there.

Wondering at such a happy situation, I asked the pastor for an explanation. He gladly gave it. For some four years the church program had included special attention to just this. Each year they had taught lessons on dating: how to get dates, good behavior on dates, how to tell when a date is no longer simply a date but is becoming something more serious, whether a date ought to become more serious or not, how to choose a life mate. Said he, "I think a pastor can do no better thing for his young people than to help steer them into happy dating and give them a Christian chance for a Christian marriage."

He told me he has much opportunity for counsel with his young people. Said he, "When a sixteen- or seventeen-year-old boy comes in to talk over his girl with me, perhaps he's about to 'break-up' or perhaps the girl has quit or maybe he feels things are becoming too serious. I give his problem just as careful attention as though he were a married man trying to save his marriage. For who knows?" he so wisely added, "I may be saving a marriage and a home before they are even made!"

Today we simply cannot dismiss these dating habits of our mid-teeners with the old-fashioned phrase "Oh, it's just puppy love!" When the physical integrity of a boy or girl is involved and there has been sex violation or all but sex violation, this is more than childish play; it is sex play. And in it there are so many elements of danger which may easily develop into the starkest tragedy.

Our mid-teen boys and girls cannot be kept apart, but they must develop a sense of separateness. The subtle sense of distance between persons without being afraid of each other—this sense is the mark of the real person. Left without any special teaching, dating loses the rewards of this unafraid, personal distance and becomes what a lad once so well stated: "We no longer court; there is no distance between us to court." Churches as well as schools should be giving *courses on the good, delightful, happy ways of courting.*

We have allowed lewd dancing and bizarre moving pictures to fix the dating habits of our youth while we have kept silent about the good, hilarious, Christian habits of dating. If schools gave the same direction to good dating and good mate-seeking as they do to producing good football teams, good glee clubs, good bands and orchestras, why should we not have something of the same finish, pleasantness, and fine achievement in good marriages and happy families?

Why not, indeed! Parents, I believe, have not been insistent enough about what church and school and community should do for their mid-teeners. I do think homes have great responsibility—but so do the church and the school and the community groups!—for healthy mingling of boys and girls of this age. There should be specific courses on preparation for marriage in our last two years of senior high school. The Atlanta, Georgia, public school system has done and is doing a beautiful piece of work in pioneering such a course required of seniors.

"May I have some spending money?" and "What about the car tonight?" are two of the questions most often debated in homes and too often with a sense of conflict on both sides. Both questions have to do with that ever insistent outside world of our mid-teeners. It is a world rather divorced from the home world in the thought of most boys and girls at this period, but they expect the home exchequer and the home garage "to come across" all the same. Parents are prone to see the home demands clearly and to "play down" the outside calls!

Our mid-teeners do need *some* money. Many have too much and many do not have enough. A farm lad said to me, "I work all the time at home. I get my clothes and board and room but I never get any spending money." I asked if he'd ever talked this over with his parents. He assured me that he had and that his parents always responded, "We just don't have it." "What they really mean," he said, "is that they haven't counted spending money for me in their budget."

He understood that his parents didn't have any too much cash but that they managed cash for the "musts" or the "necessities." He felt that *some spending money for himself* was a "necessity." "I can't even have a date," this lad went on. "I'd be willing to go out and get a job where I could earn my own spending money, but Dad needs me on the farm."

Now I honestly think this boy has a case and that his parents need to see what can be managed. He ought not to drain the family budget; he should not have more than his share; but *he should have some allowance.*

The "family car" is the second great source of family friction. A mother told me of their family's difficulties. When their son was thirteen, he found the car key and drove without permission. When pressure was put on him because he was not old enough to drive legally he merely took the family key and had a duplicate made. He is now sixteen. And his parents feel the situation is so serious that they have put their car in storage because this son has been in so many serious difficulties with older companions in the car.

One is startled to realize that fine parents have to resort to putting their car in storage all because of the problem made for them by their sixteen-year-old son. The case is extreme and unusual; let us be thankful for that. Nonetheless, more parents than would care to admit it generally are "over a barrel" as regards the family car.

Our mid-teeners do need transportation, especially boys between fifteen and eighteen. In the open country and the small town, a car is about their only way to get around. This may be a reason why some communities are pressing their school buses into more frequent use for carrying students to school activities.

Would it help if we try to set down some principles to help us here?

(1) Youths of this age should not go *on long auto trips in unaccompanied groups.* Naturally your son or daughter doesn't want to be called a "spoil-sport," and he or she might yield to pressure from the group to do things and go places *not* in the original program.

(2) The car should be used *to go and to come,* not

for driving around aimlessly. Don't these sound fair enough?

Some time ago at a state convention of the Federation of Women's Clubs a session was given to having five mid-teeners answer questions put to them by women in attendance. One of these women—a mother, by the way—asked a sixteen-year-old boy, "What would you do if *your* son took the family car with a solemn promise to use it only to drive his date to and from the place they were going, and to be in by 11:30, only to get in at two o'clock in the morning after driving 125 miles instead of the fifty miles estimated in advance?"

The lad replied, "He ought not to have the car for some time. There is such a thing as good sportsmanship toward parents."

A second one of these mid-teeners said, "He was probably just trying you out. It would be too bad if he got away with it."

All five of these mid-teeners felt that parents ought to be reasonable but that it was bad for them to allow their mid-teeners *to get away with what was not good for them.*

One girl said, "It's one thing to get mad at your parents but still respect them because you know they're right; it's quite another thing to feel they're either easy or unfair and have no respect for them."

The country over mid-teeners have too much and too free use of the "family car." But many mid-teeners need to have transportation—more parents at the wheel—and then let the mid-teeners *pile-in.* Wouldn't this be a good custom to establish?

High school graduation! No wonder that when you see your Jim and Jennie there your throat gets tight. You watch them sitting up there—Jim in a brand-new suit with his hair slicked back, and Jennie never looked prettier—well, you know then that your at-home days with them are not too many. Here you have a man-child and a woman-child soon to be out on their own. But—oh, *what a privilege to have had them under your parental roof!*

V

OUR LATE-TEENERS STILL AT HOME

This was *The Day!* An anticipated day for eighteen-year-old Bill. The dreaded day for Dad and Mother. Bill had finished his breakfast and had gone to the bathroom leaving Dad and Mother still sitting in the breakfast nook—the two dreading to get up and start the final preparations for driving Bill to the city where he was to begin his college.

They heard Bill whistling "O Happy Day!" And it didn't sound like he was whistling to keep up his courage either. Instead there was really joyful anticipation in it. Mother's eyes filled with tears as she asked, "Dad, is he really so glad to get away from home?" Said Dad as he was relating it to me later, "Bill did sound really jubilant while Mother and I had all we could do to bear up under the thought of his going away."

Of course Bill was not jubilant about leaving home. Rather he was romantically happy about his own future. This day marked a beginning of something for him—*something which held promise and destiny for him.*

High school graduation is a genuine landmark. Whether our children go to college or get a job or get married, their stay in the parental home *as a child* is over. It is a case of never again! This is a fact very difficult for parents to accept.

At this point there are two things in which later adolescents can normally be interested—vocation and marriage. Herein lies their destiny. They want a world that revolves around them as its center. They look outward and forward, not backward nor inward on their sheltering family life of the bygone years.

Further education is usually a good program for the high school graduate. Perhaps college serves as good purpose in providing them a program while they mature enough to choose a mate or a vocation as anything else. As a college teacher I have watched this growing-up process in many students while college gave them a little time to choose a mate as well as a vocation.

Many parents say to me, "I see no use or not much use in going to college until the young person has decided what he wants to do." This sounds *so* reasonable. But in fact it is *not* reasonable. For many late-teeners do not know themselves well enough to know clearly what they want to do until they are more nearly twenty or twenty-one.

They have been too busy growing bodies and *feeling themselves* to come to any very definite conscious sense of self-realization through their own capacity to work. Therefore they need a kind of proving ground—away from home temporarily but still under supervision—where they may further explore themselves and what life holds for them and have further exposures to opportunities for choice of vocations and mates. Perhaps a good college or a good training school of some other sort is the best place for this important phase of growing-up.

In college as nowhere else, later adolescents can be helped to knit together ideas and habits of feeling that will grow into a philosophy of life—a really satisfying central reason for living. Parents do not require enough of colleges where they spend their good money to send their children. The college they finally choose should be an accredited school; that is, one from which credits may be transferred to another school if the young person decides to become a doctor or teacher or lawyer or anything else which calls for graduate work.

The college chosen should have a good faculty—people who are interested in your sons and daughters as people as well as students. In my work of student counseling I have seen both good and bad atmospheres on campuses. It is usually the administration *and* the faculty which are responsible for the tone of the campus.

An education without basic principles of living does not make a good foundation for Christian living. On the other hand, a college that emphasizes only Christian atmosphere and does not have a good educational program cannot turn out good doctors or lawyers or teachers or scientists.

During that senior year in high school or perhaps even a year earlier, it is a good thing to have catalogues from colleges, to have our children talk them over with other people, to discuss colleges ourselves with others as well as with our own children. Thus, we may make the choice of a college an *important* matter and the final choice one that our young people feel is their own. Our late-teeners resent not having a share in choosing the college to which they are going. It is much easier for the colleges if their freshmen *come* rather than being *sent.*

Many church people feel quite naturally that their children *must* go to the church college. Of this I approve! But sometimes the wrong method is used and children feel they are being sent there because their parents feel that is a safe place for them to go. I believe in the church college. If it is a real college and has a nice balance of educational standards and Christian atmosphere, it is the best place in the world for our children to get an education. But, once more, they must feel that they have chosen their college. One's alma mater is really a precious possession.

Then sometimes parents are too intent on having their children go to their own college. A renowned scientist who had distinguished himself in the chemistry laboratories of his alma mater sent to his "old college" with great pride his daughter who was not at all scientifically inclined. The child was frightfully unhappy. She, who was a very bright girl, failed in some of her work and finally became so emotionally disturbed that she had to leave school.

Said she to me as I counseled her, "I wanted to go to another college and make good on my own. I simply couldn't live up to Dad's reputation on *that* campus." When I asked why she hadn't let her parents know how she felt, she replied, "I was told from a little girl where I was to go to college. I secretly sent for catalogues of other schools. But I never had the heart to disappoint my parents."

Other parents face the problem of living near a campus. It seems *so* wise to send their children near at home! It means having them under the parental roof longer and then, too, it saves money. If it works out that the college in the home town is the one to which they should go, then a very good home program is required—one that co-operates with the college.

A college dean of women had talked quite seriously with me about the problem of the "town girls." Said she, "I have no authority to control their nights out or the time they get in at night or the boys they see or the places they go." This, she thought, was definitely hard on both the dormitory and the town girls. She invited the town girls and their mothers for a conference, and we found they felt much the same way about it. The mothers were finding it difficult to exercise any authority over their daughters in college.

Finally one mother said, "When Jane started to college three years ago, we made a bargain that I was to talk with the dean, learn the rules under which the dormitory girls lived. We would observe them in our home, meantime saving money and planning that she should spend her senior year in the senior dormitory." And the plan had worked, this mother declared.

Of course, not all mid-teeners will be expecting to go to college. Many will want or have to go to work. But every parent's son or daughter needs a program after high school. There needs to be definite guidance in what they shall do and where they shall go. We may properly ask our high schools to do some special guidance and placement of their graduates who do not go to college.

To turn our children loose even to earn money without regard for their fitness to do certain things is likely to make them shiftless, undependable, and perhaps lay the foundation for failure in work. Parents can go to their pastor for help here. And I wonder if the denominational boards of Christian education ought not to give some definite help about this in Sunday school materials, in summer conferences, and in special training schools.

A mother of meager means and education but obviously of high intelligence introduced her twenty-two-year-old daughter to me. In the daughter's arms was a lovely and well-cared-for baby. After the daughter had gone, I remarked about how lovely she was.

While she finished wrapping the article I was purchasing from her, the mother said, "I knew we couldn't send her to college. She didn't make too good grades in high school, just managed to get through in many of her subjects. But in her home-making courses she made very good grades, and she loved it. She almost had to go to work after she graduated. And she wanted to go into a factory because she felt she could make more money that way to help at home.

"One day I went to a fine woman who ran a good home and who always kept help. I said to her, 'I want my Ruthie to be a good homemaker. I wish you would hire her and teach her how to run a home. I want her to do your work; but I don't want her to be just your hired girl. Might she be an apprentice with pay?' Ruthie liked the plan. She met and observed nice people. And she learned how to keep the kind of home we could never afford."

Then with justifiable pride that wise mother added, "Now my Ruthie has a good husband and a nice home of her own."

Some time ago a fine lad of nineteen who was working with one of our larger meat packing companies said to me, "I can't go to college for two reasons. First, I can't afford it. Second, I couldn't make it. But my uncle got me a job with the refrigerating department. If I could have gone to college, this is what I would have liked to study. But I couldn't have passed all the other subjects to get a college degree. I am learning practical refrigeration and I know I am making good. Perhaps I'll be as good at the practical end of it as though I had gone to college."

How different it might have been if this normal, ambitious, wholesome chap had simply been turned loose to earn money rather than working for a future!

When parents decide in all sincerity that they cannot send their children to college, they cannot in honor simply neglect to seek guidance for their search toward a good vocational future. We are not through with our children until they are equipped to earn their own living with proper pride and self-reliance. Our churches, our public schools, our community groups need to give parents practical help with their children at the time of finishing or leaving high school. It is not enough that our children merely earn a living. While doing that they should also be *earning a life of usefulness.*

Then there is always the question of what our late-teeners should do with money they earn. First, they should pay their own way if they live at home. It is extremely unwise for parents not to arrange this paying schedule. *Earning means supporting.*

Many times I have had to face husbands who have never learned that little lesson of paying their own way. Sometimes it hurts parents to face this question practically. If they want to put this money away for their children later, well and good. But each week there should be a stipulated sum turned over to the home to pay their share of living expenses. This is a matter of forming good adult habits; it should be a part of the training the home gives toward responsible living.

On the other hand, to expect our children to support us as our right is utterly selfish. I have in mind a widowed mother who had worked and supported her son through high school. As soon as he began earning, she resigned the job in which she was proficient and let her twenty-year-old son support her. She took his pay check for the support of the household as naturally as though he had been her husband. The son had met a girl whom he loved and whom he wanted to marry.

He said to me, "Mother brags on me, but it never

occurs to her that I might want a home of my own. She never seems to think that the home I am supporting is *her* home—that it can never be mine."

It was a difficult task to help this mother see how her son felt. But she finally did. She got back her old job and became a really much happier woman. As she said later, "I have now *another* home in which to visit!"

Of course, it is sometimes necessary for children to help support their parents. But this help should always be received by their parents as a sacrifice and a labor of love on their children's part, never taken as a parent's natural right. For if children were all required to "pay for their rearing," they would never get paid-up enough to support children of their own, and the world would stagnate and die.

Always, always, there is the problem of our children's getting married. Especially today more parents are wringing their hands and breaking their hearts over the *seeming* "too early" marriage of their children. And their children are experiencing a conflict here. It is a conflict growing out of many causes. Some of these are normal but others spring from very abnormal pressures.

Before the war the average age for marriage of the American girl was twenty-four, that of the boy was twenty-five. War always brings a regular epidemic of marriages. Some of these ought to be—others ought *not* to be. But war brings the question of marriage before young people. This pressure will decrease as we get further from the actual fighting. But our military training program also sensitizes our children to early marriage. Then the fact that jobs are easier to get and the pay higher for the married also urges toward younger marriage. These factors combined with the uncertain future of our boys bring early marriage sharply to our late-teeners.

The earlier "steady dating" of our high school boys and girls produces definite marriage decision earlier than we have thought good. Last year I met more high school juniors and seniors who were engaged than during any previous year. They were encountering conflict with their parents who were opposing their marriages; they were baffled by the question of managing their educational program and securing their financial support.

It is so very easy for us who are parents to say, "You are too young. You cannot marry now. You'll have to wait," and not be aware of the conflict in which these boys and girls are caught, not to see the *pressure of their world* toward marriage. *I am not arguing for early marriage!* I am only asking that we see *this* generation of late-teeners in *their* world and appreciate *their* conflict.

Many times in recent years I have counseled with high school juniors and seniors on these problems. I found their problems serious and practical; such as cannot be dismissed with a simple and final "no." They had been going together as "steadies" for two, three, or four years. Even though young in years they had become mature in their love for each other.

Maybe they had already violated their physical integrity. What to do? They really wanted to be decent. They did not want to hurt their parents. Many of them were quite aware of the educational and financial problems involved. When parents relax from their set ways and begin to see the world of turmoil and uncertainty in which their late-teeners are living, they can appreciate the practical factors in their children's problems.

Some time ago a lovely eighteen-year-old girl came to me. She was from a good family. She had been going with her young man for four years—since their freshman year in high school. He was eighteen also. They had tried to convince their parents that they should marry. They both finally came together to talk. She was with child.

When I went to her fine parents the mother's first reaction was: "I would rather you had told me my daughter was dead!" But as the father and mother faced the practical situation of this daughter they loved so dearly, they came to three very wise and definitely Christian descisions.

(1) Their daughter's marriage must be a beautiful and meaningful occasion.

(2) The boy must go on to college (he was then a college freshman—both sets of parents agreed to help with the college expenses).

(3) They (the mature parents) must understand and accept their share of the responsibility for this dilemma of their daughter—too early dating, a chaotic world, too little moral training, and their not being alert to what this lack of moral training was meaning to their very own daughter.

Parents cannot wash their hands of responsibility

for the habits of the community in which their children live; it is their children's community, their high school, their crowd. It is better to wait until the "twenties" before marrying. It is much simpler for the parents, for the late-teeners, and for the college to wait until college graduation to marry.

But it is unfair to demand that our children remain normal in an abnormal world, in a community where so many pressures are toward what is not normal. *It is for understanding that I plead*—not for license! I see the torture of these late-teeners as well as the torture of their parents. And believe me, "torture" is not too strong a word to use.

I have come to feel that early marriage is not always unwise. For example here is a nineteen-year-old lad. He is well established in a paying apprenticeship with a reliable concern. He loves very much a fine eighteen-year-old girl who is through high school and does not plan to go to college. It is far better that they marry now. They are both restless. He has had the maturing experience of two years of successful vocational experience.

Said he, "We spend so much money in dating that should be spent in buying a place and building a home for our future." He is, I think, entirely right. Yet I can understand also when the parents say, "But they are too young." Interestingly enough, the parents of this girl were married when they were exactly her present age.

Late-teeners who are not going to college and who have developed their working capacity so that they could earn a living for a home are probably better off married—*if they are sincere in their love for each other.*

As I have observed this conflict over marriage between parents and their late-teeners, I have found that parents are much more successful in exerting a good and healthy influence over their children's decision if they are willing to see the practical situation of the children before they declare too vehemently their own opinion.

True, often a late-teener through high school and not particularly challenged by any sort of post-high school program may think he is in love and want to marry *merely to have a program for living* while you, as his parents, are very sure it would never work out. Then it is much wiser to keep relaxed and openminded rather than to become manic in your attempts to break it up.

To late-teeners *declarations* from parents are very irritating. Rather the approach in the home must be with full understanding that we are dealing with a personality whose destiny is no longer tied up with that of his parents. It isn't always easy to talk over things with our late-teeners without parental insistence on telling them what *they must* do or what *we want* them to do. But even though it be hard for us to do, *what is required now is that they and we together discover what they should do.*

Many parents lose their late-teeners, not because they want to be lost, but because they have come to feel that, in order to live their own lives, they must defy their parents—to work, to marry, to live more toward their own destinies. The mother who "hangs on" too long, the father who dominates because he has been successful, these two have been responsible for many failures in work and many divorces.

The *loving* tyrants are the most *dangerous* tyrants. Often mothers who have not had sufficient of satisfying interests of their own, and fathers who have a sense of failure, seek to make careers for themselves out of their children's lives. It is wise for Dad and Mother, as they see their children growing up, to rediscover each other and to find increasing joy in their life together, to have their own interests, their own friends. For as surely as they live, their children will some time be gone and often too busy with their own lives to write home or to visit home very often.

If parents can come to see their children out in the world on their own, making their own homes, walking the floor with their own children, wrapping up sore fingers, kissing away childish fears, carving out their career and place in the world—then they can be content. And their quiet home does not echo with unbearable loneliness.

Such understanding parents will not intrude their own restlessness into the private lives of their children. Rather they will be looking into each other's heart and saying, "It has been good to live!" And reverently thanking God for the joys of parenthood, for babies, for naughty and careless childhood, for the early-teener with ungainly body and often defiant spirit, for the middle-teener declaring his independence and hurting them but not knowing how much, for the late-teeners now man and woman struggling with life on their own, and for the security in each other's love they as "Dad" and "Mother" enjoy as once again they two are together.

Yes, it is good to be a parent—and a grandparent—getting the cooky jar filled and the favorite dish all ready "for the children and grandchildren are coming home tomorrow." And then after they are gone to sit down and say, "It was so good to have them; but it's rather nice after all to feel the house quiet again and have a little time to rest."

Yes, being a parent has rich rewards if we know when to "let go," when to say, "Good-by" and "Please, come again!"

VI

GOING HOME FOR A VISIT

Jane had just come home from Maxine's. Maxine had been her best friend all through high school. Maxine was married and had just had her first baby. She was just home from the hospital. She and her husband were all agog over their first-born. As Jane watched their happiness, all at once she felt discontent. Jane had not married but was working and living at home.

When Jane arrived home that evening, for some reason nothing was right. Her mother irritated her, and her father seemed in her way. She was cross with them. Mother and Dad were hurt and baffled. This tension continued for several days. Finally, Mother could stand it no longer.

"What is wrong?" she asked Jane.

Jane flew into a temper. "What's wrong?" asked Jane, as if anybody should know. "Here I am stuck at home; other girls are either married or away on their own." With this, she burst into tears, left for her room, and shut the door.

As the mother talked this over with me, she said, "I don't know why, but when Jane shut her door, I somehow felt it was shut against me; Jane was gone."

Mother, Dad, and Jane had taken Jane's remaining at home for granted. She had seen Maxine's separateness in her own home; it brought to the surface a feeling Jane had—a resentment against her own unchanged home relationship. She felt chained —cheated; and it seemed unbearable. It had nothing to do with her love for her father or mother. She flung out at them just because they were there. It is not easy to have our children after it has come time for them normally to be away on their own. But sometimes it needs to be.

Jane bought some new things for her room—it seemed more like her own. She was encouraged to have her friends in and she was the hostess. Mother began to learn the art of sharing a home with her grown-up Jane. Dad and Mother began to recognize her as grown-up. They began to adjust to her independence and found little ways to make her feel she was an adult while she was temporarily staying at home. She was no longer just the daughter, but a person on her own in the home.

Then, there is the art of welcoming our children coming back into the home after they have been away on their first job or to college. So many parents have said to me, "When I saw him go away to school (to work, to the navy), I knew it would never be the same again." And they were right. This is the signal to begin to get ourselves ready to welcome them home for a visit.

Dad and Mother were pacing up and down the platform at the bus depot. Dick was coming home for his first visit to them since he had finished college and gotten his first job. It was eight months since they had seen him. Mother had wanted him to come by train; but he was coming by bus to save money. And now finally—here he was! With a surprisingly new maturity he shook hands with each of them—kissing Mother with real precision.

All were a little quiet as they started off in the car for home. Mother broke shortly into chatter about all the little family details that came to mind. Dick listened but gave little response. But as they sat down to the table for dinner with Uncle Bill, a change came about. For Uncle Bill was interested in the kind of work Dick was doing. Now he asked him about his job details and about new trends in that field. Then Dick talked with zest and abandonment. Dad and Mother had nothing to do but listen.

As this mother tried to analyze the situation, she said to me, "At first it certainly seemed strange. But Dad and I learned that Dick belonged to his job and was no longer just our son." Parents should not reduce their children to infantilism once they have passed that period in their lives. Perhaps it is this tendency on the part of parents that keeps Dick and Bill from coming home more often after they are out on their own. They are still our offspring but now a man-son or a woman-daughter.

Once we have granted this, then we are ready to begin rehearsing the feeling that we may actually be protected by our children now at adulthood. And if we hold ourselves in this mood, our now adultish boys and girls may the more readily take their cue from it and actually begin to play the part they should eventually hold habitually toward us. This also is one of the arts of parenthood.

Too often we hold on too long with our "greater wisdom" and "demanding hearing" merely because we are afraid our children will cease to think of us as Mother and Dad.

For so long we have felt important because they depended on us. It is a little difficult for us to make the transition to feeling that they are actually achieving adult adequacy—and that we as their parents no longer have a monopoly on all the adult adequacy in the family.

It was near the Christmas holiday. The campus is always a hectic place to be at this time. Professors become tolerant of the inattention to classroom and laboratory business. The head counselor of the college said to me, "This behavior of students just before the Christmas vacation is such a beautiful thing and so revealing!"

I asked for more on the "revealing" slant. Said he, "There is almost startling reversion to childhood; this is true of all of us at Christmastime. But," he went on, "some of these students are not going home with great pleasure. In fact, some of them are unconsciously dreading it."

He then proceeded to tell me about Bill, a sensitive, proud, brilliant boy who had worked hard to get over a feeling of inferiority because his father and mother did not get along well and were living on the edge of separation. The counselor was concerned about how much of his newly-found self-confidence Bill would lose during his Christmas vacation.

And there was Ruth, a spoiled and high-strung

lassie who was being so successful on the campus in achieving poise. Now she was going home to a "nervous" mother who wept a great deal—and who had burdened Ruth with a lonely, heartbroken letter every day she had been away—and who felt that her Ruth was not being pushed enough socially on the campus.

Said that counselor, "Many of our students will come back from their Christmas recess full of zest and ready to do a better college job. At home they will have a chance to see their parents in a different light and with increased appreciation.

"Some will come back with a better financial program and with a better slant on their study and social program on the campus because their parents are stable and wise. But others are coming back feeling defensive and hostile toward the world in general or exhausted physically and emotionally or burdened with the adult problems of their parents. These problems they are not sufficiently mature to solve—or to help their parents to a solution—and so they will worry about them."

When the counselor had finished, I could readily see what he had meant by "revealing"—he who was constantly and sympathetically working with these students on their personal problems.

Our children should leave home to go back to college feeling, "It has been good to be home with Dad and Mother; they're swell people!" They should anticipate their return to the campus with new zest because they have been in company with the homefolks.

"I am nervous as I can be!" said a mother when her son was bringing the new wife home for the first time. She had fussed and fretted as she got ready for them. Dad was a little weary of it all—said he wisely, "Mother acts as though the King and Queen were coming. I think Jack would like to come home with his new wife just for a visit. And I think she would like to be just 'family,' too." *Of course, Dad was right.*

This learning how to bring the "in-laws" in as members of the family is a needed art. In counseling I find this is one of the most difficult adjustments; it is a *must* adjustment, that is, if there are to be happy living relations. There seems to be abroad today all but a genuine phobia of in-laws. "In-law phobia" one might call it. There are a lot of heartbreaks here—entirely too many and very unnecessary ones.

It is a very foolish mother who *ever* places her son in the unhappy position of having to choose between her and his wife. For if he is determined to make a success of his marriage, he has no choice except to stand by his wife. And it is even more foolish for a wife ever to place her husband in the position to choose between her and his mother. For the husband is then likely to resent being put in such a position. This resentment may show itself in many and unexpected ways.

Parents must accept their children's marriage as final. They must accept the new son and new daughter *just* as they are! After they are old enough to marry, it is a little late for any human power to do much about changing them basically as persons. The basic acceptance of the new family members is so necessary. It is a grim fact for family living.

For parents to start tinkering with their in-laws may result in breaking them. Or they may feel forced, in order to keep their own self-respect, to defend themselves against their parents-in-law. Doing this they will develop an entirely critical attitude toward them. And this means an atmosphere in which no good feeling of fellowship can grow.

The *finality of family* is a necessity if there is to be emotionally comfortable living. "She" *is* your son's wife—mother of your grandchildren. "He" *is* your daughter's husband—father of your grandchildren. And the wedded couple must live together, must love each other completely if they are to be happy in the best sense. Wise parents will do nothing—absolutely nothing!—to hinder this. They'll do everything within their power to contribute to the happiness and togetherness of their sons' and daughters' happy family living.

Your children have always been your primary concern. Even as you awaited their coming you were asking, "Will it be a boy or a girl?" and "Will he or she be all right—sound of mind and limb?" Then after that bit of humanity came, loving care took most of Mother's waking moments and inspired Dad to earn the living for the larger family group.

Wakeful nights. Seeing children through measles, mumps, that hard cold. Dealing with that first untruth. The first little trinket you found tucked away by someone to whom it didn't belong. Getting him through arithmetic which was hard for him; getting her through her first date successfully.

No, it isn't easy to take hands off, to kiss your children's childhood good-by, to feel with full finality that they have now established a primary human institution—a family—of their own, and to understand fully that much which goes on in *that* family is "none of your business." (Excuse, *please.*) You are always interested. You are always standing by to be available. *But* you must not enter actively unless invited and then only with great care and with full appreciation that here is a family set-up separate from you though so vitally a part of you.

Because your married children are so occupied with their own affairs, they will often neglect you, forget the little attentions that would bring you such great joy. You will get hurt. Yes, but then think back. *When your children were little, did you always remember?*

Keeping good relationship with our grandchildren will pay rich and rewarding dividends. But wise grandparents *do not take over* their grandchildren. It is all right to be "sitters," to rest and relieve their parents during interludes by having the children for visits. But young fathers and mothers need to have complete charge of their own children. This helps to establish family responsibility.

Some time ago the young mother of two children came to seek counsel about difficulty she was having with her husband. I then asked to see her husband and her together. Here is the story.

When this couple's first baby came, the wife's

mother took almost complete charge of her grandson. This left the wife free; she kept up all of her social activities, but she had almost none of the *discipline of motherhood*. But young Dad had to go to work every day—late nights out did not mean *for him* that he could sleep late mornings. Then came baby number two. Grandma was finding she was not as young as she once had been. Looking after a three-year-old and a young baby at the same time proved a bit too much for her. So Grandmother suggested that a maid be employed.

Young Dad really loved his wife and family. But now he became a realist. After a bit of understanding urging he told exactly how he felt deep-down, for it was this he had kept to himself that was causing his ill temper toward his wife.

Let me put it in his own words. "Why should *my* wife want to escape the responsibility of motherhood? Why should *she* expect to still be carrying on all her social obligations? Why should her mother be the one to talk over with me what the children need? My wife is perfectly healthy! Why should it take three women, all in good health—my wife, her mother, and a maid we can't afford—to look after what other women do alone? Why couldn't our household be better adjusted to the job which I have to support my family?"

The young wife had not once even dreamed of any of all this. When she saw the picture as her husband sketched it with these questions of his—and their common sense probed deeply, the wife said, "Poor Mother! She honestly thought she was helping. Actually she was taking from us the responsibility we needed to make of us a family." And then—"What a baby I've been!"

But by then Hubby was holding her hand tenderly. She was his—not Mamma's little girl any longer. After all this, that fine grandmother had to be helped to see the total picture that was to prevail in the household from then on. I rather more than guessed that she was terribly tired and wanted to rest. But she simply hadn't learned to allow her daughter to be a woman on her own.

Hubby wanted a woman for a wife—an adult who could care for her children, not a little girl who depended on her mother to take over parental responsibility which was rightfully *her own privilege and opportunity to achieve fully rounded adulthood!* Saying good-by to the childhood of our children and acting as though we expect them to be genuine adults—we parents must master this art if there is to be deep, real happiness for all concerned.

The good God is so wise a parent. He does not manipulate us or take responsibility that we ought to carry. He gives us intelligence and opportunity. He gives us his blessing. He lets us know in so many ways that he wants us to achieve as stalwart, mature Christians. *When a crisis comes, he is always there to help us find the way through it.* If we are too hurt to carry on, he is always there —and ready.

Such times his presence gives us the only genuinely real security—such security that we can again go out to face the realities of living with new courage and hope. Here, and here only, do we parents find the final pattern for our parenthood as the perfect Parent sets our children in families of their own.

Are you sometimes afraid of the loneliness of a home when the children are all gone? Do you fear old age? Such natural fears! But lying in the background of our minds, they may so easily tempt us to do the wrong things toward our mature adult children. Without knowing quite why we do it, we may seek to hold on to our children, try to keep them dependent on us. This is the sure way to prepare for loneliness and neglect in the years to come. For if we persist in treating our grown children like ungrown personalities, they must either act the part or finally push us off to save their own self-respect.

Either of these results spells certain tragedy for aging parents. Only persons who feel adequate can be habitually generous and appreciative. We all know this, of course. But try it out on the parent-child relation. Only grown children who have been allowed to achieve adequacy can feel and act toward their aging parents with all the generosity and appreciation of which they are capable.

Life runs in its own ordained cycle. Can we not accept the entire cycle? You were young and conscious of self with development of body. You felt that separateness of person as your body became adequate to reproduce itself. Your growing sense of destiny had in it your vocation, your mar riage. You met your beloved; you romanced, courted, married.

You established your first home. The first baby was on its way—then came the arrival. What wonder and joy to be parents! You and your beloved were one in that new sense—and you were off to all the joys, the hurts, the hurly-burly of homemaking. Came the first day of school for the firstborn—then soon all were in school. And wasn't it nice to have the house quiet and to get work done without so many interruptions? But nicer still to hear the school bus stop or the romping feet on the porch. The change to play clothes—recall? And listening as to an accompaniment to: "Teacher has a pet"; "Jane thinks she is so smart!" And "Bill's going to get his tomorrow." And on occasion: "See my report card!"

Comes at last an evening when Dad asks, "Can it be that our Jack is having his first date tonight?" And another evening when Mother queries, "Dad, do you realize that Ruth is graduating from high school this spring?" How incredibly fast those teen years!"

Your Bill brings home the new wife. Ruth is in college. Dick has a job of his own. Then Dad and Mother find themselves one day at home alone. *The children come home now for visits.* The grandchildren—oh, they are so sweet. But you wonder, "Are Bill and his wife always wise with them? Now, if they were ours . . ."

And, now, if you pass this place on life's highway without yielding to its peculiar temptation, you are off to the next in life. For now we *may be wiser* than our juniors but we *must* be more understanding, more gentle, more steady in our outlooking faith. These are the outward marks of our inner learning during the parent years, that learning we shall still be using.

If we keep busy—if we always are wanting a better situation in which the young may grow up—if we somehow always expect them to do better than we have done, to accomplish more than we have accomplished—if we give those younger full opportunity to achieve—well, these are the marks of good parenthood at every stage of the parents' lives. Whether the first baby is just coming or the children are all grown and gone, keep alert to the world in which your children and your children's children must live and have their being. Don't be too ready to admit that everything from yesterday is hopelessly old-fashioned.

Don't long for the "good old days" or give up hopelessly and say that "the world is going to the devil." Above all, never *want* a rocking chair philosophy; rocking chairs so easily get to creaking if they are used too much! But always may your spirits be climbing up the golden stairs to your Heavenly Father and your eternal home.

Thank God that he made us to be parents! He chose to be Father as well as the Lord God Jehovah.